ASHLEY TURNER

FAITH
CRUSHING
FEAR

A **10** DAY DEVOTIONAL
TO FEAR CRUSHING
VICTORY

Faith Crushing Fear
Copyright © 2021 by Ashley Turner

All rights reserved. No part of this book may be reproduced or transmitted in any form or by any means without written permission from the author.

All rights reserved.
ISBN: 978-1-7372922-0-3

DEDICATION

I dedicate this book to the God who rescued my life and redeemed my soul from sin. I love you Abba!

TABLE OF CONTENTS

Foreword 7
Introduction 9
Day 1: Facing Fear 13
Day 2: Debulking The Hype 17
Day 3: My Identity Is My Weapon............... 23
Day 4: What's In You Will Show Up To The Fight 29
Day 5: The Blessing Of Borders 37
Day 6: Purpose Driven Faith Identity 43
Day 7: Uncertainty Fuels Faith? 49
Day 8: Make It Or Break It 53
Day 9: Know Your Enemy 59
Day 10: He Is Faithful That Has Promised You 63
About The Author 71

Foreword

"Faith Crushing Fear" Is a very powerful book written by my daughter in the faith Ashley Turner. I have personally watched her growth in Christ and can attest to what you are about to read in this book. I am so Godly proud of her and the person she has become. This book was birth from a real place that God so wonderfully intervened and made her whole. You will experience this very same freedom from any fear as you dig deep into this book. God bless her and continue to make His face shine upon her.

Dr. Lincoln Coffie

Introduction

Science credits fear as a bio-evolutionary response to the perception of danger that helps species to preserve themselves. Fear is usually touted as a normal self-preserving psychological response to what we perceive as dangerous or even unknown. In Psychology fear is typified through the fight or flight response that it evokes and is infamous for its ability to paralyze its victims. With such a benign description the question becomes- why is fear an enemy worth defeating?

The answer is not as simple as it may seem. When approached by this kind of query one can't retort "because the word of God says so!" We must study and seek God for the revelation of His word that sets men free. Ronald Reagan once said that "within the covers of the Bible are the answers to all the problems that men face." How do we explore those answers without drinking deeply of the wisdom of scripture? The answer is simple- we don't. We must learn to allow the

Introduction

Holy Spirit to guide us in our analysis of the word. The word is referred to in scripture as sincere milk (1 Peter 2:2) and at the same time meat (Hebrews 5:12-14). Our maturity level determines how we digest the word that we are consuming. This process of spiritual digestion, like natural digestion, breaks down masticated foods into nutrients that are useful for the body and then distributes those nutrients into the blood stream to be used by other parts of the body. Whether you are a baby in Christ who still needs milk or a mature saint who can chew the strong meat of the word; the point is clear that the word must be digested in your spirit so that the nutrients that are in the word can be distributed throughout every part of your being for your nourishment.

Humans are made of three parts: body, soul and spirit. This is so because we are made in the image of our triune God who is eternally existent as the triune Godhead: God the Father, God the Son and God the Holy Spirit. In this book it is my endeavor to expound on how fear affects every part of your being in order to expose Satan's attempt to keep you bound and God's divine plan to set you free.

Our body is responsible for receiving and translating the stimuli that we receive from our external environment. Our spirit is responsible for receiving from God what is necessary for our spiritual growth and our soul (which is made up of our mind, will and emotions) is like the control center that deciphers between the information that we receive from the spirit and the body to decide what decisions are most positively impactful to our holistic development. More aptly put- our bodies operate in triunity to accomplish even the most minute of tasks. The human conundrum is that our spirit man is always willing to do what's right but our flesh is weak (Matthew 26:41b). Often our flesh will receive information that will seat our soul into being complicit with sin. A popular singer once said that "his mind was saying no, but his body was saying yes". This may be comical to consider but it is often the very situation that we find ourselves in when an instance arises that tempts us to be fearful. If we are feeding our flesh by constantly and consistently giving in to its sinful, immoral, self serving desires we strengthen it and it's influence on our soul (mind). Through fasting, prayer and studying of God's Word we strengthen the spirit man and it's influence on our souls. The Bible says in Romans 7:25 NLT "Thank God! The answer is in Jesus Christ our Lord. So you see how it is:

In my mind I really want to obey God's law, but because of my sinful nature I am a slave to sin." I also want to take a look at how the King James Version says this verse : "I thank God through Jesus Christ our Lord. So then with the mind I myself serve the law of God; but with the flesh the law

Introduction

of sin." Many people think of strict adherence to religious law (law of Moses) as mindless ritual that without Jesus (the fulfillment of the law), doesn't accomplish the purpose of drawing us into a meaningful and intimate relationship with God. This verse highlights the reality that the law of sin is also a mindless ritual that never brings us closer to God but accomplishes it's goal of bringing about death and destruction.

God's word paired with the guidance of the Holy Spirit have given us strategy to assist our souls in making holistically beneficial decisions but, in the words of my spiritual mother Pastor Apryl, "you can't get delivered from demons that you still play with". Meaning, that it will take more than speaking in tongues, decreeing and declaring and an old fashioned tarrying service to free you from fear-your mind must be and STAY made up!

How do you keep a made up mind to live free from the grips of fear you ask? You must come out of agreement with fear and it's declarations over your life by agreeing with the word of God. As you read this book, my prayer is that you will receive revelation of the strategy that the word of God gives to be free from the grips of fear.

DAY 1

Facing Fear

What is fear? Fear is simply a mindset or belief system. I also like a definition of fear given by Pastor Michael Green who described fear by saying the "doxology of fear is the worship of negativity". It is faith in the opposite direction of what God has spoken over your life. This Fear can include all areas of our lives such as marriage, family, health, self-image, career, ministry and more. From a biochemical perspective at the onset of the perception of danger our amygdala (located in the temporal lobe of our brain) sets off a succession of bodily reactions once a threatening stimulus is perceived by our senses. These bodily reactions help us increase our ability to be efficient in danger. Some of these bodily reactions include cognitive hypervigilance (being more alert), pupil dilation (help us better utilize light to see), bronchial dilation and more rapid breathing (helps us better utilize oxygen), increased heart rate and blood pressure, and the gastrointestinal system slows down (reduces the urge to urinate or defecate during a crisis).

Fear doesn't always manifests in the face of a threat.

Fear can also manifest in expectation of a threat. This means that the threat doesn't have to be immediate, in the vicinity or a rational possibility in order to trigger these bodily responses- increasing the amount of time that fear and its bodily responses are experienced. Experiencing more heightened awareness in expectation of a threat over a prolonged period of time to the extent that it develops into paranoia is an example of how the symptoms of fear can become disruptive to an otherwise fulfilling Christian walk. Another example would be high blood pressure over an extended period could cause heart disease or stroke.

Bodily reactions to fear are a tremendous help when fear is provoked during a crisis but could be fatal if these symptoms persisted for a prolonged period of time! Although fear should not be tolerated for any period of time, its goal is the same as sin- to keep you until it destroys you. Fear is just like any other demonic spirit; it comes to steal, kill and destroy by hiding behind seemingly "normal" human instincts.

Have you ever noticed that it is generally not difficult to read a person's body language and tell what emotions they are feeling? Internationally the bodily expressions of fear are universal regardless of cultural backgrounds, generational differences or language barriers. Although shifts in emotion are easily spotted in others, many of us spend our whole lives plagued with fear and don't even know it. While the bodily manifestations of fear may vary on an individual basis there are still some very persistent and virtually indistinguishable traits that provoke wonder as to how such uniform Similarities can exist in such a diverse world. The answer is that fear is a spirit and every spirit carries with it the knowledge of how to operate in that spirit. How do we know this? Because no one had to teach you or I how to be afraid or sad. In contrast, because this applies to all spirits, we experience a greater depth of revelation of holiness and ability to live holy when we receive the Holy Ghost.

DAY 2

DEBULKING THE HYPE

Fear is a terrorist that you're going to have to fight! Early on in my Christian walk God gave me a revelation concerning the warfare that believers face. He revealed to me a scripture in the Bible which says that the kingdom suffers violence and the violent take it by force (Matthew 11:12). Then He reminded me that the kingdom is righteousness, peace and joy in the Holy Ghost (Romans 14:17). So when scripture says that the kingdom suffers violence it's not referring to a physical city or place that is under siege, but that your righteousness, peace and joy would be under attack. I believe that the Bible supports the notion that most of the enemy's attack comes through fear.

Fear has an agenda. Fear's agenda is simple: to attack your right standing with God (righteousness), wholeness (peace) and your joy (which is your strength). These areas where fear attacks are attacked because they provide an advantage over you. Righteousness or right standing is positional. The Bible says that as followers of Christ we are seated in heavenly places with Christ Jesus (Ephesians 2:6). In heaven's courtroom (where God is the judge) our sins are on trial and the entire line of defense comes from the fact that the blood of Jesus has repositioned us from death to life and from slaves to sin into being victorious over it through Christ Jesus (1 Corinthians 15:55-57). When we are seated where he is seated that means that we are spiritually located in the third heaven which is above the demonic realm located in the second heaven (Ephesians 6:12). Taking the high ground is a popular phrase because being positioned above your enemy gives you a better visual of the location and vulnerabilities of your enemies which is a strategic tactical advantage. This is important because the devil isn't under your feet unless you are seated with Christ Jesus. Only those who have received Jesus as their Lord and savior have this distinct positional vantage point. Without this vantage point the devil is over your head! Those who have not made Jesus their Lord are dead in their sins and are ruled or headed by the devil and his cohorts. Being seated with Christ also represents the authority that we have as sons of God and joint heirs with Christ.

> As joint heirs we have authority over fear through Christ Jesus.

The Bible says that the devil comes to steal, kill and destroy. Fear steals our joy, it drowns our peace in the waters of worry, and as a result destroys our faith which is a shield of defense against more attacks of the enemy (Ephesians 6:16). So fear, like any other terrorist, implements certain strategies to tighten its grip on its victims.

At a very fearful time in my life God said to me (Matthew 11:12 KJV) "… the kingdom suffers violence and the violent take it by force". During this time I was just recovering from being homeless while living with a roommate who wanted to evict me. My prayer to God was for help and relief so I wasn't expecting that response. I then asked him what does that have to do with my crisis? God then proceeded to ask me what is the kingdom? As a new believer, I was unsure of the answer; so He brought back to my remembrance a sermon snippet where a preacher quoted Romans 14:17. God showed me in this scripture that the kingdom is righteousness , peace and joy in the Holy Ghost. So when the scripture says that the kingdom suffers violence it's not referring to some celestial place in heaven that's being violently bombarded.

The scripture is saying that our righteousness, our peace and our joy suffer violence! The attacks of the enemy against our righteousness or right standing with God include using weapons of fear to attack our faith and trust in God.

> Hebrews 11:6 says that without faith it is impossible to please God.

Any place in your life where you aren't pleasing God is vulnerable to the devil and is likely to have already been taken over by his deceit that you are in right standing with God when you may not be. Jesus cautions in Luke 11:23 NLT — "Anyone who isn't with me opposes me, and anyone who isn't working with me is actually working against me".

I say this because even salvation itself starts with confessing with your mouth AND believing with your heart (Romans 10:9). So faith is seen from the onset of becoming a Christian and is an integral part of being a Christian.

Fear in many instances raises an accusation against God's faithfulness to His word. In my previous example of being in recovery from being homeless and shortly after being in danger of facing it again; through fear I had unwittingly accused God of not being with me and of not loving me. What I didn't realize is that I had allowed fear to cause me to challenge the very nature and identity of God because of my circumstances. The Bible says that God is love (1 John 4:8), so how could I be so easily persuaded that God would not be himself just to spite me and keep me homeless? He is unchanging (Malachi 3:6) no matter the circumstance. The word also says that he is with us even to the ends of the Earth (Matthew 28:20). Knowing that his word declares that He will never leave us nor forsake us (Deuteronomy 31:6) it was an affront to His deity to accuse Him of doing otherwise. If His words were not enough to calm our unbelieving hearts, God gives us a physical sign to look for in Mark 13:31 which states (NLT) "Heaven and earth will disappear, but my words will never disappear."

Even after heaven and Earth pass away we can count on God's word to stand forever.

So, the next time that you get into a fear inducing problem, ask yourself if heaven and Earth are still standing? Encourage yourself that the same God that promised you to keep you, love you and provide for you is the same God that spoke "let there be" once in the beginning and the things that he spoke to all those millennia ago have yet to cease from performing as God has commanded!

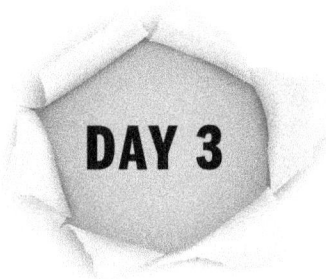

DAY 3

My Identity Is My Weapon

It is important to know that this battle you are facing against fear is apart of a larger war against the body of Christ. The best defense that you have is with faith in the word of God (Ephesians 6:17). This battle is spiritual and ultimately against the unseen things that cause the fear inducing results that we see in our physical environment.

I am reminded of a scripture that shows obedience to God, in spite of an enemy army arrayed against Israel, that made it unnecessary to physically engage in a fight that they were victorious in! 2 Chronicles 20:15-18,21-24 NLT — He said, "Listen, all you people of Judah and Jerusalem! Listen, King Jehoshaphat!

This is what the LORD says: Do not be afraid! Don't be discouraged by this mighty army, for the battle is not yours, but God's. Tomorrow, march out against them. You will find them coming up through the ascent of Ziz at the end of the valley that opens into the wilderness of Jeruel. But you will not even need to fight. Take your positions; then stand still and watch the LORD's victory. He is with you, O people of Judah and Jerusalem. Do not be afraid or discouraged. Go out against them tomorrow, for the LORD is with you!" Then King Jehoshaphat bowed low with his face to the ground. And all the people of Judah and Jerusalem did the same, worshiping the LORD... After consulting the people, the king appointed singers to walk ahead of the army, singing to the LORD and praising him for his holy splendor. This is what they sang:

....

"Give thanks to the LORD; his faithful love endures forever!" At the very moment they began to sing and give praise, the LORD caused the armies of Ammon, Moab, and Mount Seir to start fighting among themselves. The armies of Moab and Ammon turned against their allies from Mount Seir and killed every one of them. After they had destroyed the army of Seir, they began attacking each other. So when the army of Judah arrived at the lookout point in the wilderness, all they saw were dead bodies lying on the ground as far as they could see. Not a single one of the enemy had escaped."

....

Just like this passage, our warfare will be one where physical combat is not required but praise and worship is. Our praise and worship of God is an act of our faith!

Darlene Zscheche once said "to worship in the light is an act of faith, but to worship in dark is an act of war".

Fear and uncertainty are dark places that are no match for the light of God's presence. If you are ever in a dark place and you are feeling surrounded by what seems like an unassailable enemy remember what Israel did. They sought God then they praised and worshiped Him while He defeated their enemies. Their praise and worship started and finished a war that they never had to physically fight! Be reminded that this is the LORD's battle. Once you received Holy Spirit by faith and accepted Jesus Christ as your Lord and savior you were adopted into the household of faith and are now a child of God. In the same way that your children would not have to face certain things alone; whatever comes against you when you are in His will must come through God to get you because you belong to Him (see Job 1:6-22).

In warfare before any contact is made with the opponent there is usually a strategy that is drawn out by highly qualified, high ranking individuals with the intent to defeat the opposing forces. Those strategies are crafted with careful detail and tactical knowledge of every advantage and disadvantage of their opponent. This tactical knowledge may include the landscape, availability and type of weapons the enemy may possess as well as the allies who may help the opponent in a fight. The Bible was authored by the highest ranking authority in the kingdom- God. The Bible is our strategy resource and our tactical manual. Typically in physical warfare opponents are on opposite sides approaching each other to begin engaging in battle. They are on opposite sides to defend conquered territory and each side is advancing against the other side with intent to take each other's ground. Violence then ensues with a raining procession of blows from bodily appendages or from weapons in an attempt to permanently extinguish the threat of the other side's advances. Part of my reasoning in writing this book is to tell you that we are engaged in a war. Your identity as the progeny of Adam started the war but your identity in Christ is how you are equipped to fight and end the war victoriously. Our bodies are made from the dirt and every soul saved can be considered "territory" won for the kingdom of God. Our weapons of praise, worship, fasting, love, prayer, the spirit of

God, and the word of God rain down blows on the head of the enemy and pull down demonic strong holds that are encamped against us. Scripture says it this way:

....

2 Corinthians 10:3-6 NLT — We are human, but we don't wage war as humans do. We use God's mighty weapons, not worldly weapons, to knock down the strongholds of human reasoning and to destroy false arguments. We destroy every proud obstacle that keeps people from knowing God. We capture their rebellious thoughts and teach them to obey Christ. And after you have become fully obedient, we will punish everyone who remains disobedient.

....

The battle isn't just to win the souls of the unsaved but for each converted soul to be so fully persuaded that the fruit they produce from the planted, watered and matured seed of the word of God causes a ripple effect in every realm of influence that God calls them to! Our identity in Christ is our weapon against the enemy. In the book the seven mountains prophecy the author gives a powerful revelation of the seven spheres or mountains of influence that shape the culture of every nation and ultimately the minds of their constituency. These mountains are: (1) religion, (2) education, (3) family, (4) government, (5) media, (6) arts and entertainment and

(7) business. The Bible says 1 Timothy 2:2-4 NLT "Pray this way for kings and all who are in authority so that we can live peaceful and quiet lives marked by godliness and dignity. This is good and pleases God our Savior, who wants everyone to be saved and to understand the truth."

We are winning souls for Christ so that all may be saved and come to the knowledge of the truth, but we are not saved just to sit in church, dance and thank God that we are going to heaven.

 **We are praying, reading our bibles, fasting and going to church so that we may take all that we are receiving from those things to influence the seven mountains for the kingdom of God.**

Fear's hope is to leave us so paralyzed and terrorized that we don't conquer our mountains. The kingdoms or mountains of this world's system are meant to be taken over by born again believers so that Revelation 11:15 can be fulfilled which states "…The kingdoms of this world are become the kingdoms of our Lord, and of his Christ; and he shall reign for ever and ever."

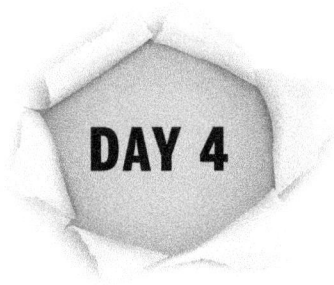

DAY 4

WHAT'S IN YOU WILL SHOW UP TO THE FIGHT

The interior of the old testament tabernacle was shaped like a cross and had four gates but only one entrance. The entryway was through the East gate. This is a distinct architectural design that contrasted any other Middle Eastern religion of its time. In order to enter into the temple gate one had to turn their back towards the sun. While this design may have been instructed by God for many reasons, it also served as an insult to the pagan worship of the "sun god". When we accepted Christ's sacrifice on the cross and received him as Lord and savior we turned our backs to worldliness, carnality, our agreement with the gods of this world and our sinful gratification of the lust of the flesh by using our bodies to do what pleases it instead of God. All that I have written up until now is so that it is clearly seen that this war involves everyone but only those who are saved have the right weapons to defeat the enemy. That's why it's so important to give your life to Christ and exchange the demonic and ungodly ways that you once operated in for sanctification and holiness. This exchange is of the utmost importance because what is in you is what will show up to the fight and Satan will not fight against himself to set you, your family or your generation free (Luke 11:18b).

Sanctification is the process through which a believer is purged and made holy and clean by the word of God, by the Spirit of God and the blood of Jesus.

Through this process we are made clean from every worldly defilement, pollutant and contaminant. Upon salvation, we become as soldiers in God's holy army and as such our uniform changes in the spirit. We are like Zechariah's account of what happened to the high priest Jeshua:

Zechariah 3:3-9 NLT — "Jeshua's clothing was filthy as he stood there before the angel. So the angel said to the others standing there, "Take off his filthy clothes." And turning to Jeshua he said, "See, I have taken away your sins, and now

I am giving you these fine new clothes." Then I said, "They should also place a clean turban on his head." So they put a clean priestly turban on his head and dressed him in new clothes while the angel of the LORD stood by. Then the angel of the LORD spoke very solemnly to Jeshua and said, "This is what the LORD of Heaven's Armies says: If you follow my ways and carefully serve me, then you will be given authority over my Temple and its courtyards. I will let you walk among these others standing here. "Listen to me, O Jeshua the high priest, and all you other priests. You are symbols of things to come. Soon I am going to bring my servant, the Branch. Now look at the jewel I have set before Jeshua, a single stone with seven facets. I will engrave an inscription on it, says the LORD of Heaven's Armies, and I will remove the sins of this land in a single day."

The Lord had instructed for Jeshua's filthy garments to be removed since they represented his sin. I would like to note that the Hebrew-Chaldee word for filthy that is used here is not seen anywhere else Biblically. It literally means soiled, as if excrementitious. Is there any thing more filthy than something that is covered in excrement or poop? While the scripture doesn't specify what has made his garments filthy, the use of this language gives a strong hint to just how filthy his (and our) sin is in the sight of a holy God. He then instructed him to be robed in clean priestly garments which represented his being made righteous. As apart of the new priestly garments given to him, a turban was placed on his head. The priestly turbans had an inscription on them that said 'holiness unto the lord' (Exodus 39:30). I believe that the turban was a representative of a mind renewal. The Bible cautions Christians to give their bodies to God and to be transformed by the renewing of their mind (Romans 12:2). The transformation from sin to righteousness isn't complete until there's a mind change. Why? Because as a man thinks in his heart so is he (Proverbs 23:7a).

The answer to every temptation to remain in sin is identity. Satan's biggest fear is for you to become who God has called you to be. That's why he is so focused on trying to stop you by allowing the spirit of fear to paralyze you into inactivity or stagnancy. One of the definitions of the word doubt is "to question". Often fear is preceded by a comparison of oneself against the perceived threat that triggers the fear response. Fear will cause you to question yourself and even God's ability to act on your behalf. When we become afraid of something we typically compare it's abilities to harm us with our ability to successfully defend ourselves from it. The fear of seeing an argentine ant, for example, would be relatively small in comparison to seeing a lion. There is usually little concern about your ability to defend yourself against an ordinary house ant but against a lion you may feel less confident that you would not be subdued. This low confidence is likely due to your mental estimation of how ineffective your human strength may be against a lion in the absence of the right weapons or protection. Every temptation starts with a miseducation of identity that leads to lusting after a perceived internal deficiency. In Genesis 3:1-6 we see a powerful illustration of a more subtle form of fear- insecurity.

> Genesis 3:1-6 NLT — The serpent was the shrewdest of all the wild animals the LORD God had made. One day he asked the woman, "Did God really say you must not eat the fruit from any of the trees in the garden?" "Of course we may eat fruit from the trees in the garden," the woman replied. "It's only the fruit from the tree in the middle of the garden that we are not allowed to eat. God said, 'You must not eat it or even touch it; if you do, you will die.'" "You won't die!" the serpent replied to the woman. "God knows that your eyes will be opened as soon as you eat it, and you will be like God, knowing both good and evil." The woman was convinced. She saw that the tree was beautiful and its fruit looked delicious, and she wanted the wisdom it would give her. So she took some of the fruit and ate it. Then she gave some to her husband, who was with her, and he ate it, too.

Insecurity is defined as uncertainty or anxiety about oneself; lack of confidence; beset with fear or anxiety. Another definition goes on to describe it as instability. What other than insecurity can so quickly cause someone who had more relationship with God than she did with the fruit of the tree of good and evil to risk it all to have an unfamiliar experience of eating the fruit? She had never tasted the fruit nor experienced the death that was sure to follow and yet with one temptation she started a domino effect that catapulted all of mankind into a level of debauchery that had never before been seen.

Notice that Eve was enticed by what she believed that she was missing out on from the unfamiliar experience of eating the fruit. The popular colloquialism for this experience is called F.O.M.O or fear of missing out. The story of Eve and the serpent is one of the earliest biblical references to one of the most effective tactics used to lure people into sin- creating a now or never moment. A pastor that I once served under said "if you ever feel like you have no other choice that is almost always a sign that it's from the devil". Why? Because love is proven by our choices. God gave Adam and Eve the option to intentionally choose Him every day that the tree of the knowledge of good and evil was in the garden. Every time that they chose to walk with Him in the cool of the day instead of disobeying His command by eating from the forbidden fruit, it was an act of love and a display of worship. The enemy is counting on our inadequately informed definition of what it means to worship. Worship comes from two words worth and ship which means to acknowledge His worthiness. We have confined the definition of worship to clapping, singing, dancing, poetic prayers and pretty words when worship is called by God to be an act of our obedience that shows we acknowledge His worthiness. What fear in you is causing you to be so insecure about your identity in Christ that you disobey what God told you? Adam and Eve's sin has shown us that one act of disobedience could cause your lineage to stay in the grips of poverty, sin, lust, etc. for generations to come. But God is worthy to be praised because in spite of the first man Adam's mistake, the second man Adam (Jesus Christ) brought life to all who were perishing in their sin (1 Corinthians 15:45).

....

Revelation 5:9-10 NLT — And they sang a new song with these words:

"You are worthy to take the scroll and break its seals and open it.

For you were slaughtered, and your blood has ransomed people for God from every tribe and

language and people and nation. And you have caused them to become a Kingdom of priests for our God.

And they will reign on the earth."

DAY 5

THE BLESSING OF BORDERS

W ho I am defines my limits, NOT FEAR. This is an important concept to grasp in order to build godly confidence. Fear is often quoted as being an acronym for: false evidence appearing real. There is a lie that you must overcome in order to defeat fear. What lies are keeping you bound in fear? Is it the lie that your not good enough? Strong enough? Intelligent enough? None of these insecurities can deny the reality that whatever God calls you to He will get you through. This is especially important to understand when defeating the fear of the unknown. Moses was a stuttering murderer (Exodus 2:12, 4:10-13) and fugitive from justice yet God told him to go back to the place where he could be prosecuted for his crimes to ask the people who raised him to set free the very slaves whose labor kept the country's economy afloat. That's a BIG ask! One that Moses felt understandably underqualified for. The command that God gave Moses not only caused generations of prayers to be answered but also caused generations of people to be freed in what would become arguably the most famous emancipation story of all time. Moses' yes wasn't to his belief in his ability to complete the task but his yes was to allow God to set His people free using Moses' obedience. Likewise, our yes to God is to allow God to work through us.

God won't force you. You must agree to let him use you. The blessing of your borders or limitations is that it creates a clear delineation between what can be accredited to your skills and abilities and what things can only be accredited to the supernatural power and grace of God. The Christian walk with God is one of an agreement with God's will that is demonstrated by our yes and is earmarked by our obedience.

Amos 3:3 "can two walk together except they be agreed."

Another rich point that we can take as believers from the story of Moses is that he said yes in spite of the apparent danger. The reality is that Moses had every right to fear retribution for killing a man but what God was proposing involved challenging the sovereignty of a king. In those days Pharaoh's considered themselves gods. In fact, in a monarchy a king's decree would go unchallenged because in a kingdom everything belonged to the king- including the people! So if Pharaoh wanted you to be beheaded there were no rebuttals. Pharaoh saw and experienced the plagues but refused to let God's people go until the very last plagued had been unleashed. Pharaoh was so addicted to the control that he had over the Israelites freedom that he ignored God's warnings. I've heard it said that fear is the currency of control. Those who have a hard time releasing control are often controlled by fear themselves. If this is you, put this book down for long enough to pray: "God I repent for my controlling and unsubmitted ways. Please forgive me, heal me and change the direction of my thinking. Help me to recognize my own vulnerability and how much I need you to guide me in every area of my life. In Jesus name amen!"

Moses said yes in the face of danger knowing that whatever he feared from Pharaoh wouldn't be as terrible as being outside of the safety of God's will. When we are in a life outside of the will of God there is much to fear. Jesus said it this way (Matthew 10:28) "fear not them which kill the body but are not able to kill the soul: but rather fear Him who is able to destroy both soul and body in hell." We must give God a yes in the face of our fears or risk the consequences.

The will of God concerning our lives is defined by our purpose. Every product has a limit which is prescribed by its manufacturer. For example, a toaster can toast a variety of food products and produce delicious results. Should the owner of a toaster go beyond the manufacturer's limitations and insert fabric or plastic into the bread slots, the toaster would destroy the items that it wasn't made for, itself and its owner. We can draw wisdom from this example and recognize that everyone has limitations based on our earthly assignment or purpose. Taking ourselves out of the context of our manufacturers prescribed use as dictated in the word of God can have catastrophic consequences. Our stories have a predetermined ending and a purpose. Whenever fear causes you to doubt your ability to perform what God has spoken about you in his word keep this in mind and state it aloud to yourself: My author predefined ??my boundaries! This reality is important in defeating fear because it replaces our emotion fueled perspectives on challenges with a heavenly perspective. An emotion fueled perspective might look at a frightening or challenging situation as an insurmountable obstacle that "someone like you" or a person of your pedigree couldn't possibly have victory over. A heavenly perspective would take refuge in scriptural promises and tell themselves that God promised to never leave them nor forsake them

(Deuteronomy 31:6) and that He would always be with them, even until the end of the world (Matthew 28:20). A heavenly perspective would say God knows the plans that he has for me and they are good not evil, but to bring me to an expected end (Jeremiah 29:11).

> Fear doesn't stand a chance in the face of God's word. That's why the Bible says let this mind be in you that was also in Christ Jesus (Philippians 2:5).

Jesus is the word. Jeremiah 51:20 calls him a battle axe and a weapon of war. Ephesians 6:17 calls Him the sword of the spirit. Hebrews 4:12 says that he is sharper than a two edged sword. These scriptures are strong assertions about the nature of whom God is. We can see the old testament foreshadowing of the then pre-incarnate Christ being depicted as the most necessary tools of defense to win any war. In the new testament we see the resurrected Christ as an invincible weapon of defense that has no rival. In the face of such overwhelming evidence of the omnipotence of God what is there to fear?

I will include a glossary of other encouraging scriptures to help you defeat fear in the back of this book.

DAY 6

Purpose Driven Faith
Identity

Fear is an enemy to faith in God. Famed author and theologian A.W. Tozier once said that "the father of fear is unbelief". It's not that fear is the total absence of faith. On the contrary, the Bible says that God has given every man a measure of faith (Romans 12:3). Fear can be seen as faith in the opposite direction of what God's word is showing you. We have to be like the two out of the twelve spies that Moses sent into the promised land who were the only ones to come out with favorable reports (Numbers 14:112). We must believe in the face of insurmountable odds by human standards, that God is greater than the odds. While everyone is believing in the power of their fears, let us choose to believe in the power of our God!

Fear is faith or belief that something or someone is dangerous or a threat. Fear is a normal response to danger but it is not a normal response to safety. There is no greater safety than is found in obedience to the will of God. The Bible says in

2 Timothy 1:7 — For God hath not given us the spirit of fear; but of power, and of love, and of a sound mind (KJV).

The Greek word for fear, δειλία (meaning timidity or cowardice), is found in that verse and is the only time that word is used in the entire Bible. What we can learn from δειλία fear is that experiences of intimidation and tests of courage may present themselves over the course of our lifetime, but don't ever make the mistake of allowing those intimidating circumstances to cause you to lose your courage to have confidence in God.

> It is our faithful obedience to God that brings about His promises, which in turn builds our confidence to keep on faithfully obeying the will of God for our lives.

> Hebrews 10:35-36 NLT — So do not throw away this confident trust in the Lord.

Remember the great reward it brings you! Patient endurance is what you need now, so that you will continue to do God's will. Then you will receive all that he has promised.

Proverbs 29:25 KJV states that "the fear of man brings a snare: but whoso putteth his trust in the Lord shall be safe". Google defines faith as complete trust or confidence in someone or something. In the first chapter we discussed that every Spirit brings with it the knowledge of how to operate in that spirit. Fear brings a snare, which is a trap that is concealed and often made enticing because it is usually surrounded by something that the prey would find desirable. Could it be that you are lured into fear because on some level you have trusted fear to provide what you desire? An example of this is found in scripture: Proverbs 22:13 NLT — The lazy person claims, "There's a lion out there! If I go outside, I might be killed!". David Guzik's commentary on this scripture sums up nicely how one might use fear as an excuse to avoid undesired activities. Guzik writes "This is the cry of the lazy man. In his imagination, the outside world and the work required to function in it are so frightening that it is best avoided.

His excuse is crazy and absurd, but such is the refuge of the lazy man". Another example of this would be an emotionally absent parent deciding that their children are physically and financially provided for well enough that their children are better off without too much emotional connection in order to mask their own fear of failure as a parent, fear of inadequacies or fear of repeating the same mistakes their parents made. Is it possible that you believed the intimidation of fear when it convinced you not to believe God?

Faith is mind over matter.

My purpose is the road map to what I should have faith for. Prayer is the action that I take to bring the seed of the word that God placed in me into germination. Germination is the process of a seed turning into a plant. When the seed is planted at the right depth in the soil, receives adequate water and is maintained at the right temperature the seed's growth process is triggered. The water activates enzymes in the seed that cause seed growth. Isaiah 61:3 says "… that they might be called trees of righteousness, the planting of the Lord, that He might be glorified." We are the planting of the Lord and in essence are as a seed. The purpose that God placed in us acts as the enzymes inside the seed that activate as soon as the water of prayer (from our high priest Jesus, our own prayers and the availing prayers of other righteous persons) connect with the word that God planted in the soil of our hearts. Our faith determines the temperature in the atmosphere of our hearts. Jesus said it this way: Very truly I tell you, unless a kernel of wheat falls to the ground and dies, it remains only a single seed. But if it dies, it produces many seeds (John 12:24 NIV). So I must pray on purpose with my purpose in mind to bring God's will into being for my life. God's will brings me to an expected end that no fear inducing circumstance has the power to derail.

Uncertainty Fuels Faith?

Faith is not necessary in the face of evidentiary certainty. The writer of Hebrews chapter 11 says that faith is the evidence of things hoped for and the evidence of things not seen. Evidence is only needed during trials. Evidence is defined as a legal term that is used to describe something that establishes facts in a legal investigation. The trials of uncertainty that you are facing require your evidence of faith in order to be turned into cases won. What we have faith in isn't our ability to have it all together or to defeat your enemies with your own strength. It's our faith in the power of the gospel which is the birth, life, death, burial, resurrection and ascension of the son of God-Christ Jesus that saved us from the accusations of the enemy which the blood of Jesus spoken of in the gospel exonerates us from (Romans 5:9). The trial is a structured process where the facts of a case are presented to a jury, and they decide if the defendant is guilty or not guilty of the charge offered. During trial, the prosecutor uses witnesses and evidence to prove to the jury that the defendant committed the crime(s). The accusations of the enemy are tried in the courts of heaven and Jesus is your lawyer. The question before the great judge is if you are guilty of breaking God's law which is revealed through His word. If it had not been for the blood of Jesus, the judgment of God against our sin would not be in our favor. Because all have sinned (broken God's law) and fallen short of God's glory- WE ARE ALL GUILTY (Romans 3:23). By all means our penalty should be an eternal place in hell.

> Galatians 3:11 says that no man is justified through the fulfilling of the law, justification comes by faith.

Justification in the legal sense is a reason acceptable to a court as to why the defendant did what he is charged with doing. None of us have any excuses before God as it relates to our fulfillment of the law's righteous requirements. The propensity to sin is a generational condition passed down from Adam (Romans 5:12-21) but it doesn't remove from us our choice in if we should disobey God or not.

Hebrews 4:2b states that the gospel preached didn't profit those who heard the message but didn't believe the message that they heard. So we can't be content with our consistent church attendance or even daily devotional reading of the word of God; however, if done correctly, both of those actions are instrumental in becoming a mature Christian and strengthening your relationship with God but they will be of no effect if you don't believe the message being transmitted through scripture.

DAY 8

MAKE IT OR BREAK IT

Considering all of the negative attributes of fear and the chaos that it causes we must recognize faith as the antithesis of the destruction that fear results in. The Bible is full of scriptures that speak on the beautiful benefits of faith . Acts 15:9b says our hearts are purified by faith. The 26th chapter and 18th verse of the same book says that we are sanctified by faith. Let's dive deeper into those terms. The term purified in the previously mentioned scripture is the Greek word katharizo which is where we get the term catharsis or cleansing. The biblical definition of the Greek term similarly means to make clean or cleanse from physical stains and dirt and/or to free from defilement of sin and from faults. The second scripture reference defines sanctified as "to separate from profane things and dedicate to God". Another definition for sanctified in that verse means "to purify by expiation (atonement): free from the guilt of sin". This is a major confirmation of the gospel message: faith in the resurrected savior Jesus the Christ purifies by atoning for your sins in a way that makes you so free of the guilt of sin that you can be/are separated and set apart for His use. All of this is possible by faith.

Faith can take you places that no natural means can bring you, such as before the presence of His glory with exceeding joy (Jude 1:24). Praise God!

The question is where does faith come from? The Bible says faith comes by hearing and hearing by the word of God. The same principle is active when we are hearing things that are against the word of God and believe them. We must guard our ears and the rest of our senses because they are a pathway to our soul (mind, will and emotions). Our senses use our neurological system to transmit information from our external environment to our brain to process what we've experienced through our senses of taste, smell, hearing, touch and sight. Because we are triune beings like our creator, we vet our experiences through our spirit (houses our connectivity to God and our awareness of the supernatural realm), soul (houses our intellect and emotions) and our flesh (houses our

5 senses and our awareness of the Earth realm). As children we are not spiritually mature enough to discern what is good for us morally or spiritually nor do we have the intellectual prowess to understand all of what our physical senses interact with, although we rely heavily on our physical senses found in our flesh. As a child we may rely on a sensation's good or bad feeling to determine if we will continue an interaction with an external stimulus or not. As we mature we are expected to be able to correctly discern the detriment and the benefit that would result from our interactions with different stimuli based on more than how good or bad it physically feels. The same is true when we are babies in Christ. Until we spiritually mature we rely heavily on what we have experienced of God through our senses. As spiritual infants many of us are drawn to God through the goosebumps and tingly feelings that we experience in His presence or the miracles that we have experienced with our eyes and other physical senses. As we mature we began to become the bride that can be guided by His eye (psalms 32:8).

While I believe this concept is easy to comprehend I would like to offer an illustration to further drive home this point. In my work with autistic and mentally ill children there are children who, despite their physical age, function at varying levels of cognition or ability to process information which may cause them to behave at the developmental level of a much younger child. Because autism is a spectrum disorder we typically classify their developmental and cognitive ability as being either low functioning or high functioning. The high functioning children are able to think and behave at a level that is closest to what is expected for their age group. The low functioning children are impaired physically and/or mentally in a way that developmentally puts them well behind their similarly aged peers.

In the natural we have certain criteria whereby we measure if a child is developing normally. This means that we must reach certain milestones by certain time periods in our lives in order to demonstrate that there are no diseases or disabilities that could impact us negatively in our future if they go unaddressed. Spiritually speaking there are certain milestones that when you meet them prove you are free from spiritual disabilities and sin sicknesses. When we first confess Christ as Lord and savior and become saved, we are a baby spiritually. We grow spiritually as we continue to consume the sincere milk of the word of God (2 Peter 2:2) via God ordained teaching congregationally, studying the word in our personal time of devotion and engaging God in prayer. Practicing these disciplines of spiritual growth causes us to meet spiritual milestones or levels of spiritual maturity. As we grow from glory to glory and faith to faith we demonstrate a mastery of understanding biblical principles, the ability to apply scripture appropriately, operate in steadily increasing levels of command over your spiritual giftings and operate with greater levels of self control. Thus, spiritual maturation contrasts from the process of physical maturation in the sense that the length of time that you are saved is not indicative of what spiritual growth milestones you meet.

The enemy is counting on using this principle to his advantage. The tactic of the enemy is to suggest sin to you in a way that appeals to your area of vulnerability. He doesn't suggest sin by saying to you "they've made you so angry you should treat yourself to a drink". No he will mimic your voice by saying "I'm so stressed I want a drink". Then he leaves the follow through to your will and emotions. That's how he sets us up to accuse us night and day before God.

....

Revelation 12:10 NLT — Then I heard a loud voice shouting across the heavens,

"It has come at last— salvation and power and the Kingdom of our God, and the authority of his Christ.

For the accuser of our brothers and sisters has been thrown down to earth— the one who accuses them before our God day and night.

....

We must resist the enemy's agenda to influence us to sin. It is then that he will flee from us (James 4:7). If we allow his advances against us to go unresisted or unchecked his advances will become more aggressive because his ultimate desire is to steal, kill and destroy John 10:10a. His ultimate desire isn't to bring you back to sin which is spiritual death or separation from God. His ultimate desire is to completely destroy you. He wants you to commit blasphemy, to become apostate and to be so addicted to sin that you chose it over God and are given over to a reprobate mind. Pastor Michael Green of Portsmouth, VA would call this committing spiritual suicide. The devil wants you to die having not fulfilled the purpose of God for your life. I imagine that he loves when people think things like "I'll give my life to God later" or when people wait until they are on their death bed to repent or give their lives to Christ. He knows that the purpose that God placed on our lives, when fully realized, actually frustrates the plans of the enemy and provides a reference point of victory so that those whom God has given us influence over can overcome demonic obstacles and defeat him (Revelation 12:11). Don't put off for tomorrow what could set a generation free today! I titled this chapter make it or break it because that phrase means leading to, or causing an outcome that will either be a total success or a total failure. As free moral agents we choose if we will follow God's will to achieve total success or the devil's agenda that will lead us into total failure.

DAY 9

Know Your Enemy

Looking more deeply into the war against the fear that comes to steal our hope of faith we should understand that fear causing circumstances are not your enemy. What you believe concerning what God placed in you to overcome the circumstance; however, may be the enemy that's causing you to live defeated. Think it not strange when these fiery trials come against you beloved (1 Peter 4:12a KJV). You were called into this fight not by the enemy but by God, therefore you will make it if you faint not.

To help you better understand why the hell that you're enduring shouldn't distract you from the victory to come, I would like to remind you of a certain shepherd boy named David who had recently been secretly anointed as the next king of Israel. Despite the calling of God on his life, the trials he endured as a shepherd that demonstrated the nobility of his character and the prophetic confirmation of his calling by one of the most anointed prophets in the whole known world at that time – David was still in the field with the sheep. Samuel had looked at all eight of David's siblings before he met David and thought that one of them would be an obvious choice as the next king. Samuel was trying to appoint who had the look, God was appointing who He called. God's appointing strategies are the same today- he looks on the heart not the outward appearance. Let us not judge others or ourselves by societally crafted notions of what God is looking for! Even if you feel that you, like David, have lived a life of obscurity until now rest assured that God is still causing the first to become the last and the last to become the first (Matthew 20:16).

David didn't immediately rise into his kingly position after the prophecy was released. The Bible even says that after Samuel anointed him that the power of God came upon David from that day forward. The power of God came upon him but he still had to leave his coronation service and go back to tending the sheep. He couldn't even brag to his friends because if anyone found out Saul would have him killed (1 Samuel 16:2-13). Does this sound familiar?

  **Has God spoken a promise over your life that you were excited about only to have to go back to your pre-prophecy reality that looks A LOT less glamorous than the prophecy?**

David even played the harp for and was an armor bearer to the man that he was going to replace. He fought a bear and a lion, killed Goliath and was on the run from the man who's death would start David's reign. My point here is that the road to manifestation of the promises of God can be tumultuous and filled with uncertainty. Although he had accomplished many things for God there were times before his accent into regality where all that he had was the memory of what God promised. God is incapable of lying. He is a man of His word and even if he spoke something that wasn't true at the moment once his word goes forth from his mouth it is so powerful that it changes the thing he spoke to into what spoke of it. As long as God's promises over his life had NOT been fulfilled David could not die. Every obstacle that he faced was not sent to defeat him but to prove the call of God on his life.

1 Peter 4:12-16,19 NLT — Dear friends, don't be surprised at the fiery trials you are going through, as if

something strange were happening to you. Instead, be very glad—for these trials make you partners with Christ in his suffering, so that you will have the wonderful joy of seeing his glory when it is revealed to all the world. So be happy when you are insulted for being a Christian, for then the glorious Spirit of God rests upon you. If you suffer, however, it must not be for murder, stealing, making trouble, or prying into other people's affairs. But it is no shame to suffer for being a Christian. Praise God for the privilege of being called by his name! So if you are suffering in a manner that pleases God, keep on doing what is right, and trust your lives to the God who created you, for he will never fail you.

DAY 10

HE IS FAITHFUL THAT HAS PROMISED YOU

Now that we have discussed the dynamics of fear and faith, let's put our faith into action by addressing fear in prayer. I have included scriptures next to each corresponding prayer point so that you can further study each scripture and seek God for revelation during your own time of prayer and devotion. God has so much in store for each of us. May your fire for God be kindled more and more with each passing day, so much so that your every fear is consumed until only faith in the power and might of God is left!

> Hebrews 10:23-25 NKJV "o Let us hold fast the confession of our hope without wavering, for He who promised is faithful. And let us consider one another in order to stir up love and good works, not forsaking the assembling of ourselves together,

as is the manner of some, but exhorting one another, and so much the more as you see the Day approaching."

THE PRAYER OF FAITH OVER FEAR

Lord Jesus I receive you as my Lord and savior. I come into agreement with your will concerning my life. I disannul every ungodly covenant and agreement that I have made with my mind, body and/or soul that was contrary to your will concerning me. Lord Jesus I ask you to take your rightful place on the throne of my heart. So, in the name of Jesus Christ I rebuke and renounce fear! I bind the works of fear that are operating in my life by the power of the Holy Ghost. God we ask that you bind the strongman of fear and spoil his house.(Luke 11) Your word says that once the thief is caught he must return seven fold of what he has taken (Proverbs 6:30-31).

I no longer yield my members to sin and fear but instead I yield my members to the God who lead captivity captive (Ephesians 4:8) and releases to me the spoils of my enemies (Exodus 3:22, 12:36)

Because my tongue is the pen of a ready writer (psalms 45:1) I decree and declare your word over my life concerning me.

I decree and declare by the power and the authority of Jesus Christ that I do not fear, for you are with me; I will not be dismayed, for you are my God. you, oh lord, will strengthen me and help me; you will uphold me with your righteous right hand.(Isaiah 41:10)

I decree and declare that When I feel afraid, I will put my trust in you.   (Psalm 56:3)

 I will not be anxious about anything, but in every situation, by prayer and petition, with thanksgiving, I will present my requests to you oh God. And your peace which transcends all understanding, will guard my heart and mind in Christ Jesus (Philippians 4:6-7)

your word declares that your own Peace is what you've left with us- your church; therefore, I will not be worried, upset or afraid because you do not give peace as the world does. (John 14:27)

God, you have not given me a spirit of fear, but of power and of love and of a sound mind. (2 Timothy 1:7) I decree and declare that I will operate from your power, your love and the soundness of mind that you have given in Jesus' name.

There is no fear in love so God I pray that you will fill me with your perfect love that drives out all fear. Because fear has to do with punishment; make me perfect in love Lord so that I will not fear. (1 John 4:18)

When anxiety tries to become great within me, let your consolation bring joy to my soul. (Psalm 94:19)

I will not fear for you have redeemed me; you have summoned me by name; I AM YOURS. (Isaiah 43:1)

An anxious heart weighs a man down, but help me attend the focus of my heart to the kind words of love that your word speaks about me and be lifted up. (Proverbs 12:25)

Even though I walk through the valley of the shadow of death, I will fear no evil, for you are with me; your rod and your staff, they comfort me. (Psalm 23:4)

You have commanded me to be strong, courageous and not terrified; or discouraged so I will obey. I choose to trust, believe and take comfort that the Lord my God will be with me wherever I go. (Joshua 1:9)

Therefore I do not worry about tomorrow, for tomorrow will worry about itself. Each day has enough trouble of its own. (Matthew 6:34)

I Humble myself then, under God's mighty hand, so that HE will lift me up in his own good time. I choose to leave all of my worries with Him, because he cares for me. (1 Peter 5:6-7)

I will tell everyone who is discouraged to be strong and unafraid! God is coming to their rescue. (Isaiah 35:4)

I will not worry about my life, what I will eat; or about my body, what I will wear. My life is more than food, and my body is more than clothes. In the face of worry I will consider the ravens: they do not sow or reap, they have no storeroom or barn; yet God feeds them! I will not worry or fear because I am more valuable to God than the birds! since my worrying can't change even the most minute detail of my life I refuse to worry but instead I choose to trust the God who has always supplied my needs even before I knew them! (Luke 12:22-26)

The Lord is my light and my salvation—whom shall I fear? The Lord is the stronghold of my life—of whom shall I be afraid? (Psalm 27:1)

I Cast my cares on the Lord and He will sustain me; he will never let the righteous fall. (Psalm 55:22)

I am strong and courageous. I will not be afraid or terrified because of my enemies, for the Lord my God goes with me; He will never leave me nor forsake me. (Deuteronomy 31:6)

For the Lord, my God, takes hold of my right hand and says to me, Do not fear; He will help me. I will not be afraid, for the Lord Himself will help me. He is my Redeemer and the Holy One of Israel. (Isaiah 41:13-14)

God is my refuge and strength, an ever-present help in trouble. (Psalm 46:1)

The Lord is with me; I will not be afraid. What can man do to me? The Lord is with me; he is my helper. (Psalm 118:6-7)

The angel of the Lord encamps around those who fear him, and He delivers them. (Psalm 34:7)

I don't worry nor am I afraid of their threats of man because even if I suffer for doing what is right, God will reward me for it. (1 Peter 3:14)

The Fear of man will prove to be a snare, but whoever trusts in the Lord is kept safe. (Proverbs 29:25)

I will not be afraid of my enemies; the Lord God himself will fight for me. (Deuteronomy 3:22)

I believe that because I prayed to the Lord, HE answers me and frees me from all my fears. (Psalm 34:4)

I will not be afraid. I will believe. (Mark 5:36) You have the final say in the face of my every circumstance.

I am thoroughly convinced that nothing can ever separate me from God's love. Neither death nor life, neither angels nor demons, neither my fears for today nor my worries about tomorrow—not even the powers of hell can separate me from God's love. (Romans 8:38-39) In this I will remain consistently confident.

The Lord God is in my midst, as a victorious warrior. He is a mighty savior.

He will take delight in me with gladness.

With His love, He will calm all my fears.

He will rejoice over me with joyful songs." (Zephaniah 3:17)

I will dwell in the shelter of the Most High and will rest in the shadow of the Almighty. I will say of the Lord, "He is my refuge and my fortress, my God, in whom I trust."…He will cover me with his feathers, and under his wings I will find refuge; His faithfulness will be my shield and rampart. I will not fear the terror of night, nor the arrow that flies by day, nor the pestilence that stalks in the darkness, nor the plague that destroys at midday. A thousand may fall at my side, ten thousand at my right hand, but it will not come near me… For He will command his angels concerning me, to guard me in all my ways…Because I love Him the Lord will rescue me; He will protect me, for I acknowledge His name. I will call upon Him and He will answer me. He will be with me in trouble, He will deliver me and honor me…" (Psalm 91:1-16)

in Jesus name, it is done! Amen!

About The Author

Ashley Turner is a southern Chicago native with a zeal for God and His people. Ashley received her bachelors degree in Psychology and Interdisciplinary Studies from Texas A&M University and is pursuing her graduate degree in Marriage and Family Therapy from Liberty University. Ashley currently lives in Harker Heights, Texas where she serves as an educator and singles ministry leader at her local assembly.

For more updates from this first time author visit:

⊕ AshleyTurnerWrites.com

✉ AshleyTurnerWrites@gmail.com

www.ingramcontent.com/pod-product-compliance
Lightning Source LLC
Chambersburg PA
CBHW031213090426
42736CB00009B/902